Swiss Cookies

Biscuits for Christmas and All Year Round

by Andrew Rushton and Katalin Fekete

Bergli
books

Published 2008 by
Bergli Books   Tel.: +41 61 373 27 77
Rümelinsplatz 19   Fax: +41 61 373 27 78
CH-4001 Basel   e-mail: info@bergli.ch
Switzerland   www.bergli.ch

ISBN 978-3-905252-17-0

Table of Contents

Introduction

I remember the moment like it was yesterday. My first Christmas in Switzerland. I had been travelling back and forth between my home in England and Zurich to visit my girlfriend and, like so many other outsiders, was struggling to come to terms with life in this undeniably beautiful but strangely impenetrable country. So her family had invited me over to spend the festive season with them and I had arrived, laden with gifts and slightly worried in the freezing, foggy and snowy Swiss winter.

When we arrived at their house, the first thing that struck me was the smells wafting out of the kitchen: a rich mixture of spices and fruits that filled the nostrils and smelled of just one thing – Christmas. Being someone who loves to cook, I ventured into the kitchen and found the family at work, chopping, mixing and rolling with the mother conducting the whole affair with her wooden spoon baton like a maestro.

The results, which we sampled after a very hearty dinner and several bottles of wine, were astonishing. Crumbly lemony Mailänderli, Spitzbuben bursting with homemade jam, Brunsli (like a brownie but not a brownie), and my soon-to-become favourites Leckerli. Suddenly my Swiss Christmas, in fact my whole Swiss experience, changed. I was in. I had helped make and eat the biscuits which to this day have become as important a part of my Christmas as roast turkey or watching the Wizard of Oz.

Biscuits (or cookies if you prefer) had never tasted like this before. Was it the strange ingredients? Was it the devil-may-care attitude to calories, cholesterol and all the other things I'd been taught to avoid? Maybe it was the way the whole family baked together pouring so much heart, soul and tradition into each one of the simple but sweet delights.

Whatever it was, it introduced me to a whole new side to the Swiss. The tradition of baking cookies, wrapping them painstakingly, and bringing them round to friends and family with an astonishingly modest shrug as if to say "these are the best I could do." And yet offering the lightest, crumbliest, spiciest homemade biscuits.

The idea to publish a book of recipes came to me later. Every year people would stop by the bookshop where I worked and ask me "where can I find out how to make those delicious Swiss cookies" and I had to shrug and say, sorry there aren't any books. So on my first day at Bergli I said, "you know what we should really publish?" and here it is.

The road to getting this book on the market has been a long and interesting one; recipes vary from canton to canton, town to town, village to village even family to family! Whilst Katalin and I were doing our research, some of our friends nearly came to blows over such details as the right way to ice Cinnamon Stars or which type of jam belongs in a proper Spitzbub. What to do? Well, we contacted the very nice people at Betty Bossi (the Swiss depend on recipes by Betty Bossi like Americans depend on those by Betty Crocker) and asked for their help, They gave us permission to use recipes from their best-selling book "New Swiss Cookies (Das Neue Guetzlibuch*) as well as from some of their other baking books. So why not have a go at recapturing those sweet Swiss Christmas moments yourself, or try out one of the other recipes included in this book and bring a taste of Switzerland into your kitchen?

Andrew Rushton & Katalin Fekete

We'd like to thank all the people who contributed excellent ideas and suggestions and helped us create this book:

Dianne Dicks
Laurent Droz
Isabelle Dürselen, Betty Bossi
Patricia Eckert
Lara Eckert
Mary Hogan
Viviane Kammermann
Moire Lennox
Catherine Rushton
Sue Rushton
Sue Style

*Guetzli is the Swiss word for cookie and is roughly pronounced goo-etz-lee or gwetslee

Before You Start

One of the most difficult aspects of writing this book was solving the differences between measurements and ingredients in Switzerland, the UK, North America and Australia, to name but a few. This is what we decided in order to make things as straightforward as possible.

Measurements
We have used grams or millilitres and cups rather than pounds and ounces or pints. If you are unsure, there are conversion tables on pages 102-104. We have often rounded amounts up or down, especially with cups, so you may need to add a little extra flour or liquid (such as milk or water) in order to get your dough to the right consistency.

Ingredients
As we have used Swiss ingredients, there are a few ground rules that cooks outside of Switzerland should follow:
- When we talk about **butter** it is always **unsalted**; extra salt can be added to taste. We have avoided margarine, although it can be used instead.
- Flour is always **plain white flour** (i.e. not self-raising) unless otherwise stated. It is advisable to sift flour before measuring.
- The Swiss use **granulated sugar** in baking unless otherwise stated.
- If you can't get **vanilla sugar**, use vanilla flavouring instead.
- The **egg** used to brush cookies before baking are usually **diluted** with some milk to make brushing easier and to give a glossier finish.
- For explanations of other ingredients, some of which you might find hard to obtain, see pages 89-93.

Utensils
A **bain-marie** (called a double boiler in the US) is a bowl placed on top of a pan of simmering water, used to slowly and gently warm or melt ingredients like chocolate.
A **spring-form baking tin** is a loose-based cake tin with detachable sides that is commonly used in baking and readily available in Switzerland.
A **piping bag** (pastry bag in the US) is a cone-shaped bag of cloth used to decorate cakes and cookies. It has a narrow opening with a nozzle at one end where you squeeze out the dough or icing.

We hope you enjoy baking our recipes. If you have any problems or want to give us feedback, then email us at info@bergli.ch.

Traditional Christmas Cookies

Christmas cookies are an important part of the festive season in Switzerland and they are served at almost every occasion. The Christmas season is a time when families and friends get together for afternoon coffee or a delicious dinner and share treats that are often homemade. There is always a wide selection of traditional Christmas cookies available.

Many Swiss still make their own cookies every year using recipes that have been handed down for generations. For many, making Christmas cookies together becomes an important family event where everybody gathers and participates; even young children help make and decorate the sweet treats.

Milanese (Mailänderli)

Makes about 80 cookies, depending on the size of the cutters		Chill dough for about 2 hours Bake for about 10 minutes

250g / 1¼ cups	**butter**	stir butter in a bowl until smooth
225g / 1⅛ cups	**sugar**	
a pinch of	**salt**	
3	**eggs**	stir in sugar, salt, and egg until the mixture is pale yellow
1	**unwaxed lemon**	grate the lemon zest and add to the mixture
500g / 3¾ cups	**flour**	fold in and mix until a dough forms, cover the bowl and refrigerate for about 2 hours
1	**egg yolk**, diluted	for brushing before baking

Method: sprinkle the work surface with flour and roll out one part of the dough 5 mm / ¼" thick. Cut out shapes with different cookie cutters, then place them on a baking sheet lined with non-stick baking paper. Chill for about 15 minutes, then brush with egg yolk. Before baking, move a fork across the cookies, pressing down lightly, or make light indentations across the top with the back of a knife (see page 97).

Baking: about 10 minutes in the middle of a pre-heated oven at 200°C / 400°F / Gas Mk 6.

Variation
with coarse sugar
Brush the Mailänderli with beaten egg white instead of egg yolk and sprinkle with coarse sugar.
Baking: about 10 minutes.

The origin of the **Mailänderli**, a lemony shortbread-type cookie, crunchy on the outside and soft in the middle, is unknown, but the name indicates that they originated in the Italian city of Milan. The original Italian version of the Mailänderli, the so-called 'biscotti Milanesi', contain candied fruits and were eaten all year round and not just at Christmas.

Scallywags (Spitzbuben)

Makes 50-60 cookies	Chill dough for 1 hour, cookies for 15 minutes, bake for 6-8 minutes

250g / 1¼ cups	**butter**	stir butter in a bowl until smooth
125g /1 cup	**icing sugar** or granulated sugar	
2 tsp	**vanilla sugar**	
a pinch of	**salt**	add the ingredients, then stir until mixture is pale
1	**egg white**	beat lightly and add to mixture
350g / 3 cups	**flour**	fold in and mix until it holds together as a dough, cover the bowl and refrigerate for about 1 hour.

Method: remove the dough from the refrigerator about 30 minutes before rolling it out. Put a portion of dough between two sheets of plastic, i.e. a clear plastic storage bag that has been cut open, and roll it out to a thickness of 2 mm / ¹⁄₁₆". Cut out pieces 4-5 cm / 1½-2" (mini-Spitzbuben 2 cm / ¾") in diameter. For half the cookies cut out the middle with cookie cutters. These will be the tops of the cookie sandwiches. Use the other half of the cookies for the bottoms, leaving cookie centres intact. Put the cookies on a baking sheet lined with non-stick baking paper, chill for about 15 minutes.

Baking: pre-heat the oven to 200°C / 400°F / Gas Mk 6 and bake for 6-8 minutes in the middle of the oven.

Spitzbuben are a shortbread-type cookie with a layer of jam sandwiched in between and dusted with icing sugar. Traditionally these cookies had three jam-filled holes to look like the face of a cheeky boy or scallywag, hence the name. The origin of Spitzbuben is unknown, but they rank high on the list of the most favourite Christmas cookies in Switzerland.

Filling

200g / 1 cup	**jelly** or jam*	warm in a pan, stirring until smooth, spread on the flat side of those cookies still with centres
a little	**icing sugar**	dust the top halves and put them on the jam-coated bottoms to make cookie sandwiches

Tip:
An easier way to roll out the dough is to put it between two sheets of a clear plastic storage bag that has been cut open, then roll it out.

Variation

Cherry Scallywags (Kirschbuben)

Kirsch filling: stir 75g / ⅓ cup butter in a bowl until smooth, fold in 75g / ½ cup icing sugar, 2 tbsp almond puree from jar and 1 tbsp Kirsch and mix properly, chill for a short time. Try using this Kirsch filling instead of jelly or jam.

*Traditionally redcurrant is used but you could also experiment with other flavours such as quince, rose hip, orange or apricot.

14

The Swiss Christmas Calendar

4th Sunday before Christmas – Advent Wreath
Make an advent wreath with four candles out of wire and wrap twigs of fir and/or of other evergreen trees around it. Decorate with pine cones, baubles or anything else you choose. Light the first candle on this Sunday, then a new candle on each of the following 4 Sundays. By Christmas Day all the candles should be lit.

1st December – Advent Calendar
Open the first door of your calendar. Open a new door each day until the last one on the 24th December. You can buy all sorts of calendars with small presents, such as chocolates or wooden animals, or pictures behind each door. But many Swiss children still get calendars of cloth or any other material that their parents have made for them.

6th December – St Nicholas comes to visit
Leave your shoes outside the door because St Nicholas is coming to visit along with his helper 'Schmutzli'* and his donkey. If you've been good, he'll fill your clean and shiny shoe with treats such as nuts, fruits, Lebkuchen (see pages 70-73), a Grittibänz (page 38) and chocolate. If you've been bad, don't expect much. St Nicholas and Schmutzli may also visit children at home in the evening. When they knock on your door, be prepared to recite a poem or sing a song. In return you'll get sweets, fruits and maybe even a present.

24th December – The big day!
Buy and decorate your Christmas tree with shining balls, tinsel or any other decoration you fancy. Many Swiss still use real candles (be very careful), although electric Christmas tree lights (and even plastic trees in different colours) have also become popular. Prepare and eat a huge Christmas dinner and wait for the Christ child to bring presents which you can open after dinner. Although some Swiss families have a traditional Christmas Eve dinner (varying from canton to canton), there is not one speciality like turkey or carp.

6th January – 'Three Kings Day' (Epiphany)
Celebrate the arrival of the 3 Kings with an Epiphany cake (see page 40).

*Schmutzli is also called 'Knecht Ruprecht' (groom Ruprecht) and is recognised in various European countries under different guises. Both St Nick and Schmutzli reportedly come from the Black Forest.

Cinnamon Stars (Zimtsterne) baked with icing (1st method)

Makes about 50 cookies, depending on the size of the cutters	Dry for 5-6 hours or overnight Bake for 3-5 minutes

3	**egg whites**	
a pinch of	**salt**	whisk the egg whites with the salt until stiff
250g / 2 cups	**icing sugar**	add the icing sugar and mix well. Put aside 100ml / ½ cup of this mixture (egg whites, salt, icing sugar) for icing later (see page 19)
1½ tbsp	**cinnamon**	
½ tbsp	**Kirsch** or lemon juice	
350g / 4 cups	**ground almonds**	add and mix together to form a dough

Method: roll out the dough either between layers of a plastic bag that has been cut open (see photo on page 14) or on a thin layer of sugar to 7 mm / ¼" thick, cut out with star-shaped cutters and put them on a baking sheet lined with non-stick baking paper.

Icing: ice the cookies with the sugary egg white mixture (see photo 1 on page 18). Leave to dry at room temperature for 5-6 hours or overnight.

Baking: pre-heat the oven to 250°C / 475°F / Gas Mk 9 and bake for about 3-5 minutes in the middle of the oven.

Cinnamon Stars are one of the most popular Swiss Christmas cookies. Their origin is unknown, but they were probably brought from Germany to Switzerland a long time ago. It seems to be an unwritten law that the cookies are always star-shaped.

Two methods of icing:

1  **Before baking the cookies:**

Spread the egg white icing with a spatula, use a wooden toothpick to spread icing into the corners.

2  **After baking the cookies:**

Briefly dip the freshly baked but cooled cookies into the plain icing.

Variations

Cinnamon Stars (Zimtsterne)
baked without icing (2nd method)
To make the dough, use 2 lightly beaten egg whites and granulated sugar instead of 3 stiffly whipped egg whites.
Method, drying and baking: as recipe page 16.

with plain icing
See page 19 and photo 2 above
with cinnamon icing
See page 19
with piped icing
See page 19

White Star Cookies (Schneesterne)
Take a portion of dough and cut out stars (see Cinnamon Stars 2nd method above).
For drying and baking, see recipe on page 16.
Decorating: decorate the cookies with plain icing or piped icing and small edible silver balls.

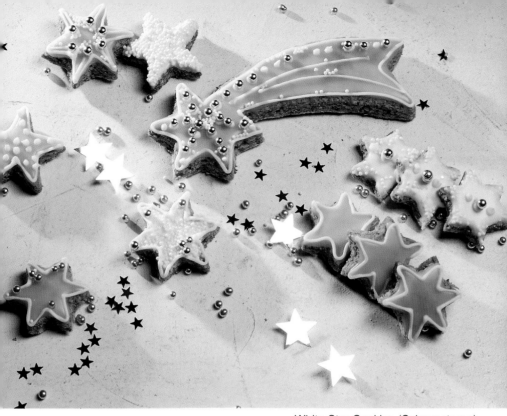
White Star Cookies (Schneesterne)

Types of Icing

Plain icing: 150g / 1⅛ cups icing sugar, 2-3 tbsp water or another liquid (see below), stir well until the icing is thick.

Cinnamon icing: add ½ tbsp cinnamon to plain icing.

Dark icing: 300g / 2¼ cups icing sugar, 100 ml / ½ cup water bring to the boil for 3 minutes stirring continuously. Then reduce to a low heat.
Put 35g / ¼ cup dark chocolate crumble in and stir until melted together.

Lemon icing: 2 tbsp lemon juice, and ½ tbsp water (optional)
Kirsch icing: 1 tbsp Kirsch and 1 tbsp water
Orange icing: 2 tbsp blood orange juice, and, if you like, ½ tbsp Grand Marnier liqueur

Piped icing: mix 150g / 1⅛ cups icing sugar with about 2 tsp egg white and 2 tsp lemon juice until you get a thick icing that can be piped easily.

Little Swiss Brownies (Brunsli)

Makes about 50 cookies, depending
on the size of the cutters

Let dough dry for 5-6 hours or overnight
Bake for 4-6 minutes

150g / ¾ cup	**sugar**	
a pinch of	**salt**	
250g / 2¾ cups	**ground almonds**	
¼ tsp	**cinnamon powder**	
1 knife point	**ground cloves**	
2 tbsp	**cocoa powder**	
2 tbsp	**flour**	mix all ingredients in a bowl
2	**egg whites**	add and mix until blended
	lightly beaten	
100g / ½ cup	**dark chocolate,**	melt in a bain-marie stirring
	crumbled	continuously
2 tsp	**Kirsch**	add Kirsch to the chocolate, then mix with the other ingredients to form a dough.

Method: roll out the dough between two sheets of plastic storage bag (see page 14) or on a thin layer of sugar about 1 cm / ½" thick. Press out with different shaped cutters and put on a baking sheet lined with baking paper. Leave to dry for 5-6 hours or overnight.

Baking: bake for 4-6 minutes in the middle of a pre-heated oven at 250°C / 475°F / Gas Mk 9.

Tip: dip the cutters occasionally in a bowl filled with sugar to be able to remove cookies from the cutter more easily (see page 96).

Variation

Orange Bars (Orangen-Brügeli)
Add grated zest of 1 unwaxed orange together with the cinnamon to a portion of dough.
Method: see above. Cut the dough into bars about 7 mm / ¼" wide and about 5 cm / 2" long.

Aniseed Cookies (Chräbeli/Anisgebäck)

4	**eggs**	
450g / 3½ cups	**icing sugar**	
a pinch of	**salt**	
1½ tbsp	**aniseed**	
1 tbsp	**Kirsch brandy**	put the ingredients in a bowl, whisk the mixture with an electric mixer for about 5 minutes until pale
550-600g / 4⅛-4½ cups	**flour**	fold in and mix to form a dough

Method: form rolls of about 1½ cm / ½" in diameter, cut into pieces about 5 cm / 2" long, make 2-3 angular incisions along the edge of each cookie and bend them slightly.

Drying: place the cookies on a lightly buttered baking sheet. Don't use non-stick baking paper. Don't move the cookies, or the effect of the incisions, i.e. "small feet", will be spoiled. Leave to dry for 24-48 hours at room temperature, making sure they are not in a draught.

Baking: bake for about 25 minutes in the lower part of a pre-heated oven at 140°C / 275°F / Gas Mk 1. Prop the oven door open with the handle of a wooden spoon and leave the door slightly ajar while baking the cookies. Let the cookies cool on the tray, then use a spatula to lift them off the tray.

1

Let the aniseed cookies dry

The aniseed cookies are properly dry if there is a white film on the bottom of the cookies.

Variations

Other Aniseed Cookie Shapes
Roll out a portion of dough on a lightly floured work surface to 1 cm / ½" thick, and cut out any shape you like with a knife or cookie cutters.
Drying and baking: see page 23.

2

Using cookie moulds with a pattern

Press the dough firmly into the mould to get a clearly visible pattern on the cookies.

Aniseed Cookies from Mould Carved with Various Designs
Take a portion of dough and add 500g / 3¾ cups instead of 450g / 3⅓ cups icing sugar.
Method: roll out the dough on a lightly floured surface to 1 cm / ½" thick. Lightly flour the mould, press a piece of dough firmly and evenly into the mould, then cut the cookies out with a knife along the edges of the mould.
Drying: see page 23. The cookies can take up to 48 hours to dry, depending on the size of the mould.
Baking: see page 23.

Did you know that ...

... using anis in baking has a long tradition and can be traced back to the Egyptians? Aniseed, both as a cooking spice and as medicine, has always been considered excellent for your health. According to Max Währen, a Swiss authority on bread-making and sweets, aniseed was used for making sweets in the Middle East in the 9th century. It was only in the 15th century that aniseed was used as a baking spice in Europe and the mention of aniseed-flavoured confectionery served as a dessert goes back to that time.

Aniseed Cookies are a speciality from the canton of Aargau and are usually part of the selection of traditional cookies that are offered during the festive season. Owing to its strong and slightly bitter taste, Chräbeli are not to everybody's liking and are said to be a 'typical' man's rather than a lady's cookie. The cookie resembles a small claw, but the name Chräbeli does not have anything to do with its shape, but simply means small thing ('kleiner Kram, kleines Zeug').

The question of where the Swiss aniseed cookie originated will most likely never be answered, as both the canton of Aargau and the German resort of Baden-Baden lay claim to the invention of this bittersweet treat. When the Swiss town of Baden became a popular spa resort, also attracting wealthy visitors from abroad, the aniseed cookie became well-known in other countries too, as guests took them home as presents.

A little less known are the **aniseed cookies** from the German-speaking part of the canton of Fribourg that look slightly different from the Baden ones but are just as delicious. They look like pinwheels and are crumbly.

Aniseed breads (Änisbrötli), typical of the French-speaking part of Fribourg, taste similar to the aniseed cookies but look quite different. Whereas the dough of aniseed cookies is pressed into moulds with designs, that of the breads is formed into rolls. These little aniseed breads are mainly eaten at the Bénichon festivals in October.

There is another beautiful traditional cookie that is eaten mainly during the Christmas season: the very thin, hard, honey-flavoured **Tirggel** displaying a beautiful picture in relief. It is a speciality from the Zurich area, but was already known in the ancient world where it was used as a sacrificial offering.

Source: Max Währen, *Gesammelte Aufsätze zur Brot- und Gebäckkunde und -geschichte, 1940-1999.*

Other Festive Bakes

Delicious Christmas bakes are an inseparable part of the festive season. Just like cookies, songs and St Nicholas, they make the festive period Christmassy and raise spirits. Wherever you go, the smell of freshly baked specialities tickles your nose and makes your mouth water. There are several traditional specialities that are eaten on a particular day during the Christmas season, like Grittibänz on 6th December or Dreikönigskuchen on 6th January, for instance. But each canton also has its own local Christmas specialities that people make themselves and would never do without: Birnbrot (Grison), Ankenwecklein (Basel), Tirggel (Zurich), Torta di Pane or Tressa (plaited chestnut bread) (Ticino) or pain de Noël and michettes (French Bernese Jura) to name but a few.

Spiced Bread (Magenbrot)

Makes enough for 2 large baking sheets	Let dough stand for 12 hours Bake for 15 minutes

500g / 3¾ cups	**flour**	
25g / ¼ cup	**Zwieback** (twice- baked bread or rusk)	grind to crumbs
1 tsp	**cinnamon**	
¼ tsp	**ground cloves**	
50g / ⅓ cup	**candied orange peel**	
50g / ⅓ cup	**candied lemon peel**	
50g / ⅓ cup	**chopped hazelnuts**	mix together in a bowl
1½ tsp	**baking powder**	
125 ml / ½ cup	**milk**	stir baking powder and milk together, then pour into the mixture above
250g / ⅔ cup	**acacia honey**	
250g / 1¼ cups	**sugar**	mix in a pan and heat to 60°C / 140°F (use meat or jam thermometer to check). Add to mixture and stir in with a spatula until a smooth dough is formed. Knead briefly, then cover and leave to stand at room temperature for 12 hours.

Method: cut into 8 pieces and roll to make logs
approx. 2 cm / ¾" thick (see photo 1 on page 30).
Lay on a baking sheet at least 4 cm / 1½" apart.

Baking: bake in the middle of a pre-heated oven at
180°C / 350°F / Gas Mk 4 for approx. 15 minutes.
Leave to cool, then cut diagonally into pieces about
2 cm / ¾" thick (see photo 2 on page 30).

	Icing:	
300g / 1½ cups	**sugar**	
100 ml / ½ cup	**water**	bring to the boil for 3 minutes stirring continuously. Then reduce to a low heat.
35g / ¼ cup	**dark chocolate**	crumble in and stir until melted together

Coating: see photo 3 on page 30.

Storing: will keep in an air-tight tin container for about 1 week

Tip: dough can be prepared 2 days in advance and kept in refrigerator.

1   Shape 2 cm / ¾" thick rolls

2   Leave baked rolls to cool, then cut at an angle into 2 cm / ¾" thick slices.

3   **Coating**: in a bowl pour a quarter of the icing mix over a quarter of the biscuits. Mix carefully with a spatula, then put onto baking paper to dry. Repeat until all are coated.

Did you know that?

The Swiss word Magenbrot, which translates as 'stomach bread', might not sound very appealing. But this traditional bake contains many spices which, in past times, were thought to aid digestion or settle an upset stomach. In the Middle Ages, only pharmacists were allowed to sell spices and food like Magenbrot. Magenbrot was originally called "Morsellen" (Gewürz-, Zucker- oder Leckerbisschen), Morsäl, Mursäl, but was renamed later.

No Swiss village fair or festival is complete without a stand selling this sweet and spicy speciality, which captures all of the flavours of winter. The village fair is still a very important occasion in Switzerland. Also called a Chilbi* in the German part of Switzerland, they usually take place around the autumn time and unofficially usher in the colder months. They usually include a fun-fair, music and dancing and stands selling all manner of things. One of the most well known and largest is the Autumn Fair (Herbstmesse) in Basel. The autumn fairs are a foretaste of the festive season when you can 'relish in its manifold sweet delights'.

As usual, food is central to Swiss festivities and the autumn fairs offer a rich variety of goodies. Look out for local cheese and sausage specialities, onion tarts and soup on the savoury side, and Magenbrot, carmelised almonds (gebrannte Mandeln), rose cakes (Rosenkuchen) and lots more besides.

*The word Chilbi has a religious heritage, originally meaning the opening or blessing of a new church.

This **pear loaf** (or literally pear bread) comes from the Grisons region and is traditionally eaten in the winter months, especially at Christmas and New Year when it is served in slices with butter or occasionally cheese on top. As with so many Swiss specialities, the recipe varies from family to family or baker to baker with each claiming theirs to be the original and best. The truth is, however, that in times past people added whatever ingredients they could lay their hands on to the autumn pears which still grow in abundance in the Grisons.

Pear Loaf (Birnbrot)

Makes 3 loaves, 600g / 1⅓ lbs each	Leave pears to soak for 12 hours Bake for 45 minutes

Filling

400g / 5⅓ cups	**dried pears**	
250 ml / 1 cup	**red wine,** preferably Merlot or Veltliner	soak dried pears in wine for 12 hours. Gently simmer for about 20 minutes until soft. Leave to cool, removing any stalks or pips. Drain, keeping any left-over wine.
150g / 1 cup, each of	**dried figs** **prunes**, stoned **dates**, stoned	chop together with pears into fine pieces, a food processor or similar is ideal, put into a bowl. You can also add the left-over wine from the pears.
100g / ⅔ cup	**raisins**	
100g / ⅔ cup	**sultanas**	
100g / ¾ cup	**candied orange peel**	
100g / ½ cup	**cane sugar**	
1	**unwaxed lemon**	grate rind, add zest to mixture
1 tbsp	**Lebkuchen spices**	(see page 91)
1 tsp	**cinnamon**	
200 ml / 1 cup	**Kirsch** or **Williams**	
100 ml / ½ cup	**rosewater** (see page 93)	mix together with pears etc.
1.3 kg / 3 lb	**Zopf dough** (using 750g / 5¾ cups flour, see recipe page 35)	add 500g / 1lb of the dough to the fruit mixture and knead. This is your fruit dough.
100g / ⅔ cup	**hazelnuts**, whole	
100g / ⅔ cup	**almonds**, whole	
100g / ⅔ cup	**walnuts**, whole	knead into the fruit dough
1	**egg yolk**, diluted	for brushing

33

Method: cut the fruit dough into 3 equal parts and shape into logs about 20 cm / 8" long. Cut the Zopf dough also into 3 parts and roll out into a rectangle approximately 30 x 25 cm / 12 x 10". Lay the log-shaped filling in the middle, then wrap the outer Zopf dough around the filling, brushing with egg or water to seal. Prick several times with a fork and trim off any excess dough.

Baking: bake in the middle of a pre-heated oven at 200°C / 400°F / Gas Mk 6 for approx. 45 minutes.

Storing: if wrapped in clingfilm or in a freezer bag, the pear loaf keeps in the refrigerator for approximately 1 month.

1   Lay the filling in the middle of the rolled out dough and cut out the corners.

2   Brush the edges of the dough with egg or water and wrap around the filling.

Zopf is a plaited bread made from plain flour. It used to be a typical Christmas bread but has become the bread many Swiss enjoy for their Sunday breakfast.

Its origin goes back to the 14th century when bread bakers' guilds were formed in many cities. Even in those days the bakers' creativity knew no boundaries, which led to interesting creations such as the plaited Zopf. Despite its increasing popularity, bakers were restricted to making and selling the Zopf bread only during the festive season, from St.Thomas' Day (21st December) until Epiphany (6th January), because baked goods made with flour were considered a luxury at that time.

Source: Max Währen, *Gesammelte Aufsätze zur Brot- und Gebäckkunde und -geschichte, 1940-1999.*

If you fancy making a **Zopf** for your next Sunday breakfast, you need the following ingredients:

500g / 3¾ cups	**flour**	
4g / ½ tsp	**dried yeast** (or 10-15g of fresh yeast)	
about 1½ tsp	**salt**	mix in a bowl
300 ml / 1¼ cups	**milk**, lukewarm	
50g / ¼ cup	**butter**, melted and lukewarm	
½	**egg**, beaten	add the butter to the mixture and knead until a dough forms. Leave to stand until the dough rises to twice its original size (about 30 minutes).
½	**egg**	for brushing before baking

Method: divide the dough into two parts and form 60 cm / 24" long rolls. Then plait the bread.

Baking: pre-heat the oven to 200°C / 400°F / Gas Mk 6 and bake in the middle for 30-45 minutes.

Bread Cake (Torta di Pane)

Makes 1 cake serving 8 people	Allow bread mixture 12 hours to soak
	Bake for 2¾ hours

250g / ½ lb	**stale white** or	
	brown bread	remove crusts, then dice
100g / 1½ cups	**Amaretti** biscuits	crumble, mix together in a bowl
1l / 4¼ cups	**milk**	
1	**vanilla pod**, cut	bring to the boil, then pour over
	lengthwise	the bread. Leave to stand for
		12 hours. Remove the vanilla
		pod. Mash the mixture with fork.
250g / 1⅔ cups	**sultanas**	
100g / ¾ cup	**candied orange peel**	
2 tbsp	**Grappa**	mix together and leave to mari-
		nate for several hours. Add to
		bread mixture.
75g / ⅓ cup	**dark chocolate**	grated or finely chopped
100g / ¾ cup	**chopped almonds**	peel before chopping
1	**unwaxed lemon**	grate zest and add
1 tsp	**cinnamon**	
¼ tsp	**mace** or nutmeg	add to mixture
3	**eggs**	
75g / ⅓ cup	**sugar**	beat together until thick and
		foamy. Fold into mixture. Pour
		into a spring-form or round cake
		tin 24 cm / 9½" in diameter.
50g / ⅓ cup	**pine nuts**, whole	sprinkle on the top
a little	**icing sugar**	for dusting after baking

Baking: pre-heat the oven to 150°C / 300°F / Gas
Mk 2 and bake for 2¾ hours. When done leave to
cool before transferring to a cake rack. Dust with icing
sugar before cutting. Can be kept refrigerated and
wrapped in tin foil for 1 week.

St Nicholas Bread (Grittibänz*)

Makes 4 medium-sized Grittibänzen

Let dough rise for about 35 minutes
Bake for about 25 minutes

500g / 3¾ cups	**flour**	
1½ tsp	**salt**	
3 tbsp	**sugar**	
6g / 1 tsp	**dried yeast**	mix together in a bowl
	(20g fresh yeast)	
60g / ⅓ cup	**butter**, cut into	
	pieces and softened	
300 ml / 1¼ cups	**milk**, lukewarm	add, mix, then knead for 10 minutes until dough is smooth and pliable. Cover and let stand for about 2 hours until double in size
1	**egg**, beaten	for brushing later
	hazelnuts, almonds and **raisins**	for decorating

Method: cut dough into 4 pieces and make 4 longish rolls. Then cut in each roll for arms, legs and neck (see photo on page 39). Place on a baking tray lined with baking paper, then brush with beaten egg and decorate.
The dough is basically the same as the traditional Swiss Sunday bread Zopf (see page 35).

Baking: for about 25 minutes in the lower part of a pre-heated oven at 180°C / 350°F / Gas Mk 4. Remove from the oven and let cool on a cake rack.

Once it has cooled, you can decorate your Grittibänz further, e.g. with coarse sugar, flaked almonds, or pieces of cloth, ribbons, etc.

* pronounced Grit-tee-baenz in the canton of Zurich

Did you know that?

The **Grittibänz**, or Grättimaa in Basel, is a sweet white bread roughly formed into the shape of a man with currants for eyes and coat buttons and some-times decorated with coarse sugar. Some children prefer to make St Nicholas breads in the form of aeroplanes, houses or funny figures. It is traditionally eaten in the German-speak-ing part of Switzerland on 6th December, St Nikolaus Day. The name comes from the old Swiss German words 'Gritte' or 'Grittle', meaning bow-legged. And 'Bänz', a shortened form of the name Benedict, was once so common in Switzerland, it also came to simply mean a man. Therefore a Grittibänz is a bow-legged old man.

The tradition of giving out bread in strange shapes on 6th December can be traced back to the middle ages when Swiss children were given either a horn-shaped bread roll or one made to look like a woman. Over the years this woman became a man and the name Grittibänz was coined for him in the 19th century. At that time they were up to 60 cm / 24" long and sometimes made from a Lebkuchen dough (page 71).

Epiphany Cake (Dreikönigskuchen)

Makes 1 cake serving 8-10 people

Let dough rise for about 40 minutes
Bake for 40 minutes

500g / 3¾ cups	**flour**	
1½ tsp	**salt**	
2 tbsp	**sugar**	
1 tsp	**vanilla sugar**	
2 tbsp	**honey** (runny)	
6g / 1 tsp	**dried yeast**	mix together in a bowl
	(20g fresh yeast)	
60g / ¼ cup	**butter**, softened	
250 ml / 1 cup	**milk**, lukewarm	see the method for Grittibänz on page 38
2	**egg yolks**	
1	**egg yolk**	for brushing
some	**water**	

Dough: the dough is very similar to that of the Grittibänz and is based on the traditional Swiss Sunday bread Zopf (see page 35) but contains more sugar and/or honey, making it sweeter.

Method and baking: cut ⅔ of the dough into 8 portions and roll into balls, 'hide' your king figure in one of the balls (see page 41). Roll the last ⅓ into 8 smaller balls and arrange the smaller balls around the inside. Brush with diluted egg yolk and let rise at room temperature for 40 minutes before baking on a buttered baking sheet for 40 minutes in the middle of a preheated oven at 200°C / 400°F / Gas Mk 6.

Tip: use a spring-form or round cake tin approx. 26 cm / 10" in diameter.

Epiphany Cake
(Dreikönigskuchen)

Epiphany Cake is a sweet white bread with dried fruit, decorated with coarse sugar and flaked almonds. It's traditionally eaten on 6th January. The cake usually has a large roll in the middle and smaller rolls around the outside, one of which contains the figure of a king. Whoever gets the roll with it, is crowned King or Queen for the day. You can make a decorative crown yourself. In times gone by, people used to hide a bean, coin or metal button in the cake, but nowadays it's usually the figure of a king made of a hard, non-toxic plastic. As most Swiss are expecting to find a king in their cake, accidents are few and far between – most of them happening to unsuspecting newcomers!

The tradition of a special January feast with the naming of a king for the day can be traced back to Roman times and the celebration on 6th January as Three Kings Day or Epiphany to the 9th century. However, the Epiphany cake as we know it today is a recent invention and was introduced in the post-war years by an innovative Swiss master baker.

Biscuits for All Year Round

Switzerland may be famous for its traditional Christmas cookies, but you can indulge your sweet tooth all year round. Some deep-fried bakes like Fasnachtschüechli, Öpfelchüechli, Rosenchüechli, Schenkeli, Schlüferli, Schlüfküchlein (Beignets soufflés), Zigerkrapfen or the savoury Fastenwähe are made and served only at Fasnacht*, but many other bakes are on offer all year round. There are many stores and magnificent and renowned cafes that offer an impressive selection of delicious sweets and pastries, ranging from cookies in all shapes and sizes to heavenly chocolate treats and cakes – one is simply spoilt for choices.

Many Swiss people like baking and they keep a supply of all sorts of treats which they love to share with friends.

*Fasnacht is the Swiss equivalent of Carnival or Mardi Gras, the festivity that symbolises the beginning of Lent.

Lemon Moons (Zitronenmöndchen)

Makes about 50, depending on the size of the cutters	Leave to dry for 5-6 hours or overnight Bake for 8-10 minutes

350g / 4 cups	**almonds,** peeled and ground	
200g / 1 cup	**sugar**	
1 pinch	**salt**	mix together in a bowl
2-3	**unwaxed lemons**	grate rind and add zest to mixture
1½	**fresh egg whites,** lightly beaten	add and mix to make a dough

Method: roll out dough between two sheets of a clear plastic storage bag (see page 14) or in a thin layer of sugar until approximately 7 mm / ¼" thick. Press out various size moons with a cutter and place on grease-proof paper on a baking tray. Leave at room temperature to dry out (5-6 hours or overnight).

Baking: pre-heat the oven to 160°C / 325°F / Gas Mk 3 and bake in the middle for 8-10 minutes.

Decorating: after baking, brush the Lemon Moons with warm lemon icing (see page 19); add thinly sliced lemon zest or roasted flaked almonds to the icing while still moist.

Tip: try using unpeeled instead of peeled almonds to give a slightly bitterer flavour.

Variation

Orange Moons (Orangenmöndchen)
Use unwaxed orange instead of lemon zest and an orange icing (see page 19).

Vanilla Horns (Vanillehörnchen)

Makes 55-60 cookies	Cool dough 30 minutes, chill again before baking, bake 10-15 minutes

250g / 1½ cups	**flour**	
a pinch of	**salt**	mix together in a bowl
200g / 1 cup	**butter**	carefully rub into the flour with cold hands until the mixture has formed into crumbs
75g / ½ cup	**icing sugar**	
10g / 2 tsp	**vanilla sugar**	
100g / 1⅛ cups	**ground almonds**	add and form to a dough. Cover and leave to stand in a cool place for 30 minutes.

Method: keeping the remaining dough in a cool place, roll out, a little at a time, into finger-thick pieces, 2 cm / ¾" long. Rub these pieces between your palms until they are a little thicker than a pencil. Shape into a crescent and lay on a baking tray lined with baking paper. Let cool for 15 minutes before baking.

Baking: pre-heat the oven to 200°C / 400°F / Gas Mk 6 and bake in the middle for 10-15 minutes. Remove from baking tray with care, so the cookies don't break.

Vanilla sugar

6 tbsp	icing sugar	
15g / 3 tsp	vanilla sugar	mix together and dust over the cookies while they are still warm

Tip: if the dough is too dry, add a tablespoon of milk or a bit of lightly beaten egg white.

Variation

Vanilla Pretzels (Vanillebretzeli)
Instead of making horns, form the dough into a pretzel shape.

Sablés Shortbread (Sablés)

Makes around 60 cookies	Chill for approx. 30 minutes Bake for 10-12 minutes

175g / ¾ cup	**butter**	soften in a bowl
75g / ⅓ cup	**sugar**	
1 tsp	**vanilla sugar**	
a pinch	**salt**	
1 tbsp	**milk**	add to the butter and stir until the mixture is light in colour
250g / 1¾ cups	**flour**	add and mix until a dough is formed

Method: make 2 rolls about 3-4 cm / 1-1½" in diameter, wrap in clingfilm and chill for approx. 30 minutes or put in the deep freeze for a few minutes. Cut rolls into slices 5 mm / ¼" thick and place on a baking tray lined with baking paper, generously spaced apart. Bake immediately and put remaining dough in fridge.

Baking: pre-heat the oven to 200°C / 400° F / Gas Mk 6 and bake for 10-12 minutes.

Variations

Tuscan Sablés (Toscana-Sablés)
Add 100g / 1⅛ cups ground pine nuts or walnuts to a portion of dough before folding in the flour.
Decorating: garnish with pine nuts or halved walnuts before baking. Once cooled, dust with icing sugar.

Jackstraw Sablés (Mikado-Sablés)
Before folding in the flour, add 50g / ⅓ cup finely chopped candied peel.
Decorating: once baked, lightly brush the cookies with lemon icing (see page 19) and garnish with finely chopped candied peel.

Variations of Sablés (continued)

Chocolate Sablés (Schokolade-Sablés)
Before folding in the flour, add 2-3 tbsp cocoa powder to a portion of dough.
Decorating: dust the cookies with cocoa powder or brush them with dark
chocolate icing (see page 19) while they are still warm from the oven.

Double Sablés (Doppelte Sablés)
Halve some of the chocolate sablés before baking. Leave the cookies to cool
before joining the halves together with some dark cake icing and icing them.
Garnish with candied peel such as orange, lemon or angelica.

Black and White Cookies: Duo and Rings (Schecken)
Duo Sablés (1): cut both doughs in half, shape the dark
dough into two rolls of about 3 cm / 1¼" in diameter and the
white dough into two 2 mm / ¹⁄₁₆" thin squares, brush with a
little egg white, put dark dough rolls on top of the white
rectangles, then roll them up together.

Ring Sablés (2): cut both the white and the dark dough in
half, then roll them out into equal-sized squares approx.
2 mm / ¹⁄₁₆" thin. Brush the white dough with some egg white
and place the dark dough on top of it, then roll them.

50

Black and White Cookies (Schwarz-Weiss-Gebäck)

Applies to all four variations:
Duo, Rings (see page 50)**, Chessboard and Marble Sablés**
Take a portion of sablés dough and a portion of chocolate sablés dough.
See page 48 for method and baking.

Chessboard Sablés (Schachbrett-Sablés) (3):
Cut dough into three parts. Take two parts and form bars of
1½ cm / ⅔" in diameter. Roll out the third part into a thin
rectangle. Lightly brush the bars with a little egg white, join
them together, then place them on the lightly brushed
square and wrap around.

Marble Sablés (Marmor-Sablés):
When making black and white cookies, whether duo, rings
or chessboard, there may be some dark and white dough
left. Press the remaining dough together and form a roll to
make marble sablés.

Macaroons (Makrönchen)

Makes about 50 cookies

Let cookies dry for 5-6 hours or overnight
Bake for 8-12 minutes

Hazelnut Macaroons (Haselnuss-Makrönchen)

3	**fresh egg whites**	
a pinch of	**salt**	whisk until stiff peaks form
100g / ½ cup	**sugar**	add half the sugar, continue to whisk the mixture until shiny
300-350g / 3⅓-4 cups	**ground hazelnuts**	fold in the hazelnuts and the remaining sugar

Method: use two teaspoons to shape the macaroon cookie mixture into small piles or oval shapes (see photo 1 below), or fill the mixture into a piping bag and squeeze it through the big star-sized nozzle (see photo 2 on page 54).

Decorating: garnish each cookie with a hazelnut. Let biscuits dry at room temperature for 5-6 hours or overnight.

Baking: pre-heat the oven to 180°C / 350°F / Gas Mk 4 and bake the macaroons in the middle of the oven for 8-12 minutes.

Forming macaroons

1
Use two teaspoons to form small piles or oval shapes.

2  Fill half the piping bag with macaroon mixture, hold the bag firmly with your hand and make sure the nozzle is fitted properly, pipe cookies in whatever forms and shapes you like (rounds, rings, drops, fingers, etc.).

Variations

Almond Macaroons (Mandel-Makrönchen)
Take one portion of dough and add almonds instead of hazelnuts.
Decorating: with peeled and halved almonds before letting the cookies dry.

Pistachio Macaroons (Pistazien-Markönchen)
Take one portion of dough and add 250g / 2¾ cups peeled, ground almonds and also about 75g / ¾ cup ground pistachios instead of hazelnuts.
Decorating: garnish with pistachios before letting the cookies dry.

Macaroons are round, almond-flavoured cookies that are light, fluffy and soft, and moist in texture. They are closely related to the meringue and are said to have originated in Italy where they're called amaretti.

Presenting and Packaging

In Switzerland some people don't just bake for the fun of it, they bake to impress their friends with what they have produced. Often the way a gift is wrapped and presented is more important than the gift itself. This is especially true of Christmas cookies; so if you are planning on making them into a gift, you should let your imagination run wild. Here are a few ideas should you need them:

In a box or a tin: take a plain white box and decorate the lid yourself or have your children do it. Paint the lid and leave to dry, then weave different coloured ribbons across the top. Finish off with a bow and/or some holly leaves.
Gift-wrapped: wrap in conventional wrapping paper before adding silver or golden stars, glitter or similar. Finally, wrap the whole thing in a coloured mesh.
In a cone: take a rectangular-shaped doily and cut a piece of gift wrap to cover the middle, leaving the lacy edges free. Stick down. Roll into a cone shape and fill with cookies.
In a bag: buy or make a gift bag out of thick coloured paper. Use coloured cord for the handles.
Other things to add: finish off your Christmas gift with candles, mini-baubles, golden wire or cord, stickers, holly, fir twigs, cookie cutters or similar.

Crunchy Cookies (Grüschbrötli)

250g / 1¾ cups	**flour**	
a pinch of	**salt**	mix the flour and salt in a bowl
125g / ⅔ cup	**butter**	rub into the flour with cold fingertips until crumbly
200g / 1 cup	**sugar**	
1 tsp	**cinnamon**	
1	**unwaxed lemon**	add grated zest
125g / 1½ cups	**ground almonds**	add and mix the ingredients
1	**egg**	
2-3 tbsp	**milk** or water	fold in and form a dough
1	**egg**, beaten	for glazing before baking

Method: roll out the dough on some flour or non-stick baking paper into a rectangle, about 5 mm / ¼" thick. Transfer dough with baking paper to a baking tray, brush with egg. Move the back of your knife diagonally and crosswise over the dough, pressing it down lightly to make a criss-cross pattern.

Baking: bake for 15-20 minutes in the middle of a pre-heated oven at 220°C / 425°F / Gas Mk 7. Cut into 4 x 4 cm / 1½ x 1½" squares and lift off with a spatula.

Tips:
- Replace cinnamon by Birnbrot spices (see page 92).
- Add zest of 1 unwaxed orange and 2-3 tbsp orange juice instead of lemon zest and milk.

Variations:
- **with a hole pattern:** brush dough with egg and prick it with a fork.
- **with a striped pattern**: brush dough with egg and move a fork diagonally across.
- **double-decker**: put some raspberry jam on two cookies, then sandwich them together.

Walnut Cookies (Baumnussguetzli)

Makes about 50 cookies

Refrigerate dough for about 1 hour
Bake for about 10 minutes

175g / 1⅓ cups	**flour**	
100g / 1⅛ cups	**ground walnuts**	
125g / ⅔ cup	**sugar** or cane sugar	
a pinch of	**salt**	mix together in a bowl
75g / ⅓ cup	**butter**, melted and slightly cooled	
1	**egg**	
1 tbsp	**rum**	add the ingredients and mix until a dough forms
1	**beaten egg**	reserve for brushing later
a few	**walnuts**	whole, halved or chopped, for garnishing the cookies

Method: form the dough into two rolls, each about 6 cm / 2½" in diameter. Roll them in cane sugar and wrap in clingfilm before refrigerating for about 1 hour or deep freezing a few minutes. Cut the rolls into approximately 3-4 mm / ⅛" thick slices, then transfer the cookies to a baking tray lined with non-stick baking paper.

Garnishing: brush with beaten egg and decorate with walnuts.

Baking: pre-heat the oven to 200°C / 400°F / Gas Mk 6 and bake for about 10 minutes in the middle of the oven.

Orange Rounds (Orangentaler)

Makes about 70 cookies	Refrigerate dough for about 45 minutes Bake for 12-15 minutes

175g / ¾ cup	**butter**	beat in a bowl until soft
125g / 1 cup	**icing sugar**	
a pinch of	**salt**	add, stir until the mixture is pale
1	**unwaxed orange**	add grated zest and 2½ tbsp juice
2-3 tbsp	**almond puree***	add orange and almond puree
350g / 2⅔ cups	**flour**	fold in and mix to form a dough

Method: form the dough into two rolls, about 5 cm / 2" in diameter, then wrap in clingfilm and chill for 45 minutes or briefly deep freeze. Cut rolls into 3-4 mm / ⅛" thick slices and place on a baking tray lined with baking paper. You could try cutting out a triangle and pasting it on to a slice again with a squirt of orange icing (see page 19).

Baking: bake for 12-15 minutes in the middle of a pre-heated oven at 180°C / 350°F / Gas Mk 4.

Garnishing: brush cookies with orange icing (see page 19) after baking. To decorate, use thinly sliced orange zest, cut into long thin strips.

Tip: instead of forming rolls, try rolling out the dough and cut out different shapes with the cutters.

Variation

Heart-shaped Orange Rounds (Herztaler)
Cut small hearts out of the sliced dough with a cookie cutter, bake and then place them on the wet icing.

*You should be able to find jars of almond puree at your local health food store.

Ginger Crescents (Ingwer-Kipferl)

Makes about 40 cookies

Chill dough for about 1 hour
Bake for about 10 minutes

100g / ½ cup	**butter**	beat in a bowl until soft
75g / ¼ cup	**pear concentrate** (see page 90) or acacia honey	
1 tbsp	**water**	add both ingredients, then stir into the mixture
1	**unwaxed lemon** grated zest	
2 tsp	**ground ginger**	
a pinch of	**salt**	
75g / ¾ cup	**ground hazelnuts**	
25g / ⅛ cup	**buckwheat flour**	
125g / 1 cup	**wholemeal flour**	add the ingredients and mix until the dough comes together. Cover the dough and put in the fridge for about 1 hour.

Method: take a portion of dough and shape it into rolls about as thick as your finger. Cut them into pieces of about 2 cm / ¾" in length and make pencil-thick rolls (see page 97). Then form into crescent shapes or twists and place on a baking sheet lined with non-stick baking paper. You can brush the cookies with diluted egg yolk and sprinkle with unrefined cane sugar.

Baking: pre-heat the oven to 180°C / 350°F / Gas Mk 4 and bake for about 10 minutes in the middle of the oven.

Lebkuchen & Biberli with Lemon Grass Marzipan

Makes about 50 cookies

Chill the dough for about 13 hours
Bake each tray for about 8 minutes

Lebkuchen dough

200g / 1½ cups	**flour**	
1 tsp	**Lebkuchen spices** (see page 91)	
1	**lime**, rinse with hot water, dry, use grated zest of ½ lime	mix together in a bowl
100g / ¼ cup	**acacia honey**	
40g / ⅓ cup	**icing sugar**	
1 tbsp	**water**	warm mixture in a pan, stirring continuously, then pour into the bowl
1 tbsp	**milk**	
1 tsp	**baking powder**	dissolve baking powder in milk and add to the mixture. Knead to a smooth and pliable dough, let the covered dough chill in the refrigerator for about 12 hours
a little	**cream**	for brushing

Method: roll out the dough on a lightly floured surface, about 7 mm / ¼" thick. Cut out shapes with cookie cutters, then brush with cream.

Baking: see page 72

To make **Biberli**, use Lebkuchen dough and fill it with Lemon Grass Marzipan (for method and baking, see page 72).

> **Biberli** is a traditional cake from the mountainous canton of Appenzell, the smallest of all Swiss cantons. It uses the same dough as the popular Lebkuchen but has a marzipan filling.

Lemon Grass Marzipan

150g / approx. 1 cup	**peeled almonds,** whole	
2-3	**lemon grass stalks**	cut the soft inner layers into small pieces
50g / ¼ cup	**white chocolate,** crumbled	finely chop and put in a bowl
50g / ⅛ cup	**acacia honey**	
½ tbsp	**lime juice**	add and knead the mixture thoroughly

Method: roll out the Lebkuchen dough on a lightly floured surface into a rectangle (about 20 x 30 cm / 8 x 12"). Cut lengthwise in two halves, brush the edges lightly with water. Cut the marzipan into two halves and form into 2 logs (about 30 cm / 12" long and 2 cm / ¾" in diameter). Lay one log on the longer edge of the dough. Roll the dough around the marzipan so that it is well wrapped, leave to chill for about 1 hour. Roll the second log in the same way. Cut at an angle diagonally across the roll into pieces approximately 3 cm / 1¼" thick to give a rhombus shape. Place the Biberli on a baking sheet lined with non-stick baking paper before brushing them with cream.

Baking: bake for about 8 minutes in the middle of a pre-heated oven at 200°C / 400°F / Gas Mk 6. Take them out of the oven and transfer them with the baking paper onto a rack, then brush the Biberli again with cream and leave to cool.

Lebkuchen (see page 71)

Variation

Biberli with Hazelnut and Cinnamon Filling
(Biberli mit Haselnuss-Zimt-Füllung)

For making the Biberli, see pages 71-72.
Filling: 150g / 1 cup **whole hazelnuts**, 1 tsp **cinnamon** powder and 50g /
¼ cup **milk chocolate**, crumbled, then finely cut in the food processor.
Add 100g / ½ cup **sweetened condensed milk** and 1 tbsp water, then
knead until the dough is firm and compact.

Storing: the filling can be kept in a closed container for about 1 week.

Glarus Turnovers (Glarner-Täschli)

Makes about 24 cookies   Bake for 12-15 minutes

2 rectangular	**puff pastry sheets** (about 42 x 25 cm / 16½ x 10" each)	halve 1 pastry sheet lengthwise and lay out on a lightly floured work surface
1	**egg**, lightly beaten	lightly brush the pastry sheet

Filling

about 300g / ⅔ lb	**Birnenweggen** filling (see page 92)	put heaped teaspoon of filling at regular intervals on one half of the pastry sheet
a few	**almond slivers**	sprinkle on filling, fold the other half of pastry sheet over and brush the edges with a little water, then cut out rectangles

Decorating: make incisions on the upper pastry layer with a sharp knife or cut the edges with a pair of scissors. Place on a baking tray lined with baking paper.

Baking: bake for 12-15 minutes in the middle of a preheated oven at 220°C / 425°F / Gas Mk 7.

a little	**icing sugar**	dust the cookies when cooled

Tip: Brush with the remaining egg before making incisions and baking instead of dusting with icing sugar after baking.

Variation

Almond-filled Turnovers (Mandel-Täschli)
Use almond mixture or almond paste (see page 89) instead of Birnenweggen filling (see page 92). Also add some chopped, dried apricots and roast the almond slivers.

Swiss Doughnuts (Zigerkrapfen)

Makes 12 doughnuts   Leave to cool for 1 hour

Dough

250g / 1¾ cups	**flour**	
2 tbsp	**sugar**	
½ tsp	**salt**	mix together in a bowl
125g / ⅔ cup	**butter** (cold)	slice into small pieces and rub into the flour with your hands until you have a breadcrumb-like consistency
125g / ½ cup	**sour cream**	add and mix (don't knead) until you have a smooth dough. Press down flat and leave to stand in a cool place for 1 hour

Filling

150g / ⅔ cup	**Ziger (or ricotta)**	
4 tbsp	**sugar**	
¼ tsp	**cinnamon**	
100g / 1⅛ cups	**ground almonds**	
3 tbsp	**raisins**	
½-1 tbsp	**lemon juice**	mix together in a bowl

Method: Roll out dough to a rectangle (30 x 40 cm / 12 x 16"), 1½ cm / ½" thick. Cut squares 10 x 10 cm / 4 x 4". Spoon the filling into the middle of the squares. Brush the edges with a little water and fold to form triangles. Push down the edges with a fork to seal.

Frying: In a deep fat fryer, heat the oil to 170°C / 325°F. Put the doughnuts in a few at a time and fry until they are golden brown on both sides. Once done allow to cool slightly on kitchen paper before rolling in a sugar and cinnamon mixture.

Tip: The dough can be made up to ½ day in advance if refrigerated or the deep-fried doughnuts can be made a day in advance and heated up before serving.

Leckerli

200g / 1 cup	**sugar** or cane sugar	
a pinch of	**salt**	
4	**eggs**	mix in a bowl and stir until pale
1 tbsp	**Birnbrot spices** (see page 92)	
1	**unwaxed lemon**	grate zest
60g / ½ cup	**candied orange peel**	chop
60g / ½ cup	**candied lemon peel**	chop
250g / 2¾ cups	**ground hazelnuts**	
60g / ¼ cup	**butter**	melt, leave to cool then add and mix together
250g / 1¾ cups	**flour**	fold in until the dough comes together

Method: spread the mixture about 1 cm / ½" high on a baking tray covered with baking paper.

Baking: bake for 20-25 minutes in the middle of a pre-heated oven at 180°C / 350°F / Gas Mk 4.

Kirsch Icing:

150g / 1¼ cups	**icing sugar**	
1 tbsp	**Kirsch** or lemon juice	
2 tbsp	**water**	mix well, then spread on the Leckerli straight from the oven

Decorating: scatter chopped candied orange peel over the wet icing.

Cutting: cut into rectangles approx. 4 cm / 1½" wide and 5 cm / 2" long before they cool. Halve the rectangles lengthwise to get smaller Leckerli cookies.

Note: the cookies taste even better after 1-2 days. For storage tips see pages 100-101.

Chocolate

The Swiss are inseparable from their chocolate; whilst other nationalities may love Swiss chocolate, they can't hold a candle to the sweet-tooth world champion Swiss who put away over 10 kg / 22 lb per person of the dark brown stuff per year!

Cocoa may have arrived in Europe as early as the 16th century (Columbus is often credited with its introduction), but the Swiss love affair didn't begin until the early 19th century when Cailler set up his first factory near Vevey.

Thereafter, the Swiss and their chocolate have been defined by high quality and innovations: chocolate that melts, milk chocolate and nutty chocolate – just a few of the household versions that the experimental chocolatiers of Switzerland invented and marketed.

Many of the world-famous Swiss chocolate dynasties live on today and their names still set the mouth watering. Cailler, Tobler or Suchard remain strong brands despite becoming part of global conglomerates, whilst other household names, such as Lindt & Sprüngli are still family owned. Within the country, however, a lively mix of traditional and innovative chocolatiers thrive. Next time you are in Switzerland, a visit to Teuscher or Sprüngli in Zurich, Graf in Basel, Tschirren in Bern or any one of the hundreds of other small chocolate shops should be high on your list of things to do, so as to see for yourself that the Swiss are still enjoying experimenting and making the best chocolate in the world.

In the German-speaking part of Switzerland you will often see the word chocolate written in local dialect Schoggi, not 'Schokolade' as in high German – this is pronounced 'shock-ee' and may come in very useful.

Chocolate Balls (Schokoladenkugeln)

Makes about 70 balls	Stand for 5-6 hours or overnight Bake for 2-3 minutes

3	**eggs**	
250g / 1¼ cups	**sugar**	mix together in a bowl until the mixture is light in colour
200g / 1½ cups	**chocolate powder**	add to the mixture and stir in well
300g / 3⅓ cups 2-3 tbsp	**ground almonds** **corn flour**	add to the mixture and mix to a firm dough. Cover and leave to cool for about 1 hour

icing sugar, cocoa
or **chocolate powder** for decorating

Method: shape the dough into walnut-size balls and roll in the icing sugar or cocoa powder until coated. Place on a baking-paper covered baking tray, generously spaced apart. Leave to stand for 5-6 hours or overnight so they can dry out.

Baking: pre-heat oven to 250°C / 475°F / Gas Mk 9 and bake for 2 minutes. Keep a careful eye on them during baking as the smaller balls may already begin to melt after 2 minutes. Should this happen, remove the balls from the oven immediately! Allow them to cool slightly before removing from the paper. The finished balls should be hard on the outside but still soft and gooey in the middle.

Decorating chocolate balls:

Pour cocoa or chocolate powder onto a deep plate or soup bowl.

Swiss Chocolate Truffles (Truffes)

Makes about 25 truffles

Cooling 1-2 hours

200g / 1 cup	**dark chocolate**	break into a bowl
50 ml / ¼ cup	**cream**	
50g / ¼ cup	**butter**	heat together in a pan, pour over the chocolate, stir together until all the chocolate has melted. Leave to cool.
1 tbsp	**cognac**	add to the mixture and whisk in until the chocolate mass lightens in colour and is smooth. Cover and leave for 1-2 hours in the fridge to set.

Method: pour cocoa or chocolate powder onto a deep plate or soup bowl. With a teaspoon, scoop up the truffles mixture. Form into balls with your fingers then roll in the cocoa powder until coated before transferring to paper praline cups. Dip your hands regularly in cold water to cool them down and dry them thoroughly. You may need to chill the truffles again before serving.

Storing: the truffles will keep for 3 days if refrigerated. They can also be frozen and stored for 3-4 weeks.

Variations:
– Use milk or white chocolate instead of dark.
– Instead of cognac, try using a shot of espresso coffee, Amaretto, Cointreau, champagne, Grand Marnier, Kirsch, rum, whisky, Williams, or 1 tsp vanilla sugar, cinnamon, ginger or cardamom.
– Instead of rolling the finished truffles in cocoa, try using icing sugar, ground hazel nuts, walnuts, almonds, or pistachios, finely chopped candied or dried fruits.

Toblerone Brownies

50g / ¼ cup	**butter**	melt in a pan
200g / 1 cup	**dark Toblerone**	break into small pieces, add to butter, stir over a low heat until melted. Leave to cool slightly.
2	**eggs**	
100g / ½ cup	**sugar**	
1 tsp	**cinnamon**	
a pinch of	**salt**	stir together in a bowl until well mixed. Add the chocolate and blend together.
50g / ⅓ cup	**walnuts**, roughly chopped	
75g / ½ cup	**currants**, soaked in 2 tbsp of dark rum	
75g / ½ cup	**flour**	stir into the chocolate mixture. Pour into a greased baking tray, approx. 20 x 20 cm / 8 x 8" and spread out evenly.

Baking: pre-heat oven to 180°C / 350°F / Gas Mk 4 and bake for approx. 20 minutes. To determine if they are ready, test with a toothpick to be sure the brownies are still moist inside. Leave to cool slightly but cut in the tin whilst still warm. Leave in the tin until completely cooled before removing.

Decorating: dust with cocoa powder, coat with icing and/or decorate with rosettes of chocolate or silver sugar balls.

Tips:
- Brownies will keep for about 1 week if stored in an air-tight container and refrigerated.
- Brownies can be frozen and stored for 6-8 weeks, and taste great if they are not completely thawed!

Variations:

Classic Brownies (Brownies)
Use dark chocolate instead of Toblerone. Omit the currants, using an extra 50g / ⅓ cup of roughly chopped walnuts instead and swap the cinnamon for vanilla sugar.

Mocca Brownies (Mokka-Brownies)
Use mocca-flavoured chocolate instead of Toblerone. When melting the chocolate, add 2 tbsp of cognac and a shot of espresso. Try using roasted pine nuts instead of walnuts.

Orange Brownies (Orangen-Brownies)
Use the regular Brownie recipe but before adding the flour, mix in 200g / ¾ cup of orange marmalade and 2 tbsp of Grand Marnier liqueur. Decorate with candied orange slices dipped in melted chocolate.

Whities
Use 200g / 1 cup white chocolate instead of dark chocolate and add 3 tbsp of cream. Try using chopped almonds instead of walnuts.

Whilst Brownies can lay claim to being the American tray bake number one, their popularity has risen in Europe too and by swapping regular chocolate for Toblerone you can give your Brownies a Swiss touch.

Guide to Ingredients

Names of the ingredients are given in English, German and French.

Almond paste, Mandelmasse / Backmarzipan, pâte d'amande / massepain
Almond paste or marzipan is used mainly in Europe to form decorations for cakes and cookies. It is a mixture of almonds, sugar and a liquid such as cane syrup, and is similar to marzipan but less granular and less sweet.

Amaretti biscuits   Amaretti   Amaretti
These small, slightly bitter almond cookies are similar to macaroons and were originally produced in Italy but are now also made in the canton Ticino. They contain almonds, sugar, egg white as well as bitter almonds or bitter almond extract, hence the name which means 'little bitter things' in Italian.

Butter   Butter   beurre
Butter in Switzerland (as in most of continental Europe) is usually unsalted, assume this is the case unless the packaging tells you otherwise.

Butter	Butter	beurre
Clarified butter	Kochbutter	beurre de cuisine
Salted butter	gesalzene Butter	beurre salé

Chocolate   Schokolade   chocolat
Switzerland without chocolate just wouldn't be the same (see page 80) and there are many different varieties available, the most common being:

Chocolate with hazelnuts	Gianduia	gianduja
Cooking chocolate / coating chocolate	Kuvertüre / Couverture	chocolat de couverture
Milk chocolate	Milchschokolade	chocolat au lait
Plain chocolate / dark, bittersweet or semi-sweet chocolate	Zartbitterschokolade	chocolat noir
	Edelbitter	chocolat noir amer
	Cremant (which can be very high in cocoa solids)	Cremant
White chocolate	weisse Schokolade	chocolat blanc

Eggs   Eier   œufs
Whenever possible, use organic, free-range eggs.

Free-range eggs	Eier aus Freilandhaltung	œufs d'élevage en plein air

89

Guide to Ingredients

Flour   Mehl   farine

In Switzerland flour used in baking is always plain, finely ground, wheat flour unless otherwise stated. The Swiss use a plethora of wholemeal flours (including graham, spelt or other whole grain flours) which, if finely ground, can be used instead of plain flour to make cookies. Zopfmehl, the flour used to make the traditional Sunday bread, is also readily available, containing 10-15% spelt and finely ground and giving a more elastic consistency.

Plain / all-purpose	Weissmehl	farine fleur / blanche
Wholemeal	Vollkornmehl	farine complète
/ whole-wheat		

Self-raising / self-rising flour isn't available in Switzerland. Use plain flour instead and add 10g / 2½ tsp baking powder to each 225g / 1⅔ cups flour.

Honey   Honig   miel

The Swiss often use honey as an alternative sweetener to sugar. This can produce delicious cookies which are generally lighter in colour and softer in texture. Be careful when using honey with a strong flavour or those which are very dark in colour as they can be overpowering. We recommend using the lighter acacia honey for baking. Substitute approx. 4 tbsp of honey for every 100g / ½ cup of sugar.

| Acacia honey | Akazienhonig | miel d'acacia |

Nuts, Nüsse, noix

Almonds	Mandeln	amandes
Hazelnuts	Haselnüsse	noisettes
Pinenuts	Pinienkerne	pignons de pin
Walnuts	Baumnüsse (Walnüsse)	noix

Flaked	Blättchen / gehobelt	effilé
Ground	gemahlen	moulu
Slivers	Stifte	bâtonnets

Pear concentrate   Birnendicksaft   concentré de jus de poire

In order to make pear concentrate, take small, extremely aromatic pears and wash and crush them. Then clarify, filter and deacidify the juice before making a concentrate out of it. You don't need to add any sugar, additives or preservative as the concentrate is already very sweet.

90

Guide to Ingredients

Schnapps   Schnaps   alcool

Schnapps is a general term for liquors or spirits distilled from fermented fruit or vegetables. In Switzerland many farmers use up fallen fruit or unsold fruits in this way. Although it is illegal in Switzerland to produce large quantities of homemade schnapps, some farmers will take excess fruit and do the job for you. The most popular kinds of schnapps, which can be used to flavour all manner of cookies and chocolates are:

Cherry schnapps	Kirsch	kirsch
Mirabelle schnapps	Mirabellenschnaps	alcool de mirabelle
Pear schnapps	Williams	alcool de poire
Plum schnapps	Zwetschgenschnaps	alcool de pruneau
Quince schnapps	Quittenschnaps	alcool de coing

Other liqueurs used in Swiss baking:

Cointreau	Cointreau (Orangenlikör)	cointreau
Grand Marnier	Grand Marnier (Orangenlikör)	Grand Marnier

Spices

The key flavours used in Swiss cookie baking are:

Aniseed	Anis	anis
Cinnamon	Zimt	cannelle
Lemon	Zitrone	citron
Vanilla	Vanille	vanille

Alongside these there are a few other spices you should make sure you are well stocked with:

Cardamom	Kardamom	cardamome
Cloves	Nelken	clous de girofle
Ginger	Ingwer	gingembre
Nutmeg	Muskatnuss	muscade

Lebkuchen Spices

It is a mixture of spices used primarily for Lebkuchen (page 71) but also for biscuits requiring some spice. Although the mixture varies, the following should provide an adequate substitute if you can't find the real thing:

2 tsp ground ginger	Ingwer	gingembre
1 tsp ground cinnamon	Zimt	cannelle
¼ tsp ground nutmeg	Muskatnuss	muscade
¼ tsp ground cloves	Nelken	clous de girofle

Guide to Ingredients

Birnbrot Spices (Birnbrotgewürz)
By adding some extra spices to Lebkuchen spices you can create your own spices for making Pear Loaf (page 33) and other recipes:

½ tsp cardamom	Kardamom	cardamome
¼ tsp coriander	Korinader	coriandre
¼ tsp mace	Macis	macis

Birnenweggen filling (Birnenweggen-Füllung)
It is a Swiss speciality used for making Glarus Turnovers (page 75) and other similar sweets. it is a pear mixture sold in tins, but you can also make it yourself. The closest comparison would be mincemeat (which can be used as a substitute) although without suet or other fats. Although the recipe varies from region to region, the basic ingredients are:

Dried pears	getrocknete Birnen	poire séchées
Dried figs	getrocknete Feigen	figues séchées
Sultanas	Sultaninen	sultanines / raisins secs
Candied lemon	Lemonat / Orangeat	écorce de citron
/ orange peel		/ d'orange confits

Some kind of alcohol, Kirsch, Williams or plum schapps

Aniseed	Anis	anis
Cinnamon	Zimt	cannelle
Nutmeg	Muskatnuss	muscade
Pepper	Pfeffer	poivre

Sugar   Zucker   sucre
Listed below are the most common types of sugar used in baking. Be aware that the Swiss often bake with what they call Brauner Zucker or Rohzucker (literally brown or raw sugar) which we've translated as cane sugar. Despite its brown colour, Rohzucker isn't the same as brown sugar used in baking in North America, which is moister and stickier than cane sugar and isn't available in Switzerland.

Cane	Brauner Zucker	sucre de canne
	/ Rohzucker	
Caster / superfine	Streuzucker	sucre en poudre
Decorating / coarse	Hagelzucker	sucre en grains
Demerara	Farinzucker	cassonade
Granulated	Kristallzucker	sucre cristallisé
Icing / powdered	Puderzucker	sucre glace
Vanilla	Vanillezucker	sucre vanilliné

Guide to Ingredients

Yeast   Hefe   levure
Most Swiss use fresh yeast (in cubes) (Frischhefe) when baking cookies and
cakes, but you can also use dried instant yeast, which you can find at any
grocery shop. When using dried yeast (Trockenhefe) instead of fresh yeast
(Frischhefe), you need to be a bit more patient as it takes a bit longer for the
dough to rise.

Some other ingredients you might find useful

Baking powder   Backpulver   poudre à lever
Baking powder is usually used in baking, but you can also find baking soda
(Natriumbikarbonat) at the pharmacy. Triebsalz or Hirschhornsalz, is another
raising agent that can be used instead of baking powder and that you can
also get at the pharmacy.

Candied lemon / orange peel	Lemonat / Orangeat	écorce de citron / d'orange confits
Cornflour / cornstarch	Maisstärke, e.g. Maizena (a brand name)	amidon de maïs
Currants	Korinthen	raisins de Corinthe
Icing / glazing	Zuckerguss, Glasur	couverture de sucre glace
Jam	Konfitüre	confiture
Lemon	Zitrone	citron
Lemon peel or zest	Zitronenschale	zeste de citron
Milk	Milch	lait
Orange	Orange / Apfelsine	orange
Pear	Birne	poire
Raisins	Rosinen	raisins secs
Rosewater	Rosenwasser	eau de rose

Rosewater is made from roses and used to flavour food. It is available at
any grocery shop.

Sultanas	Sultaninen	sultanines / raisins secs
Zwieback	Zwieback	Zwieback

Zwieback is a brand name for a twice-baked bread and very similar to rusk.

Tips for Making Dough

Basic but important tips
- Read the recipe carefully, assemble all the baking utensils and set the measured ingredients aside.
- Before you start a recipe, you may want to get the oven and baking sheets ready, i.e. pre-heat the oven and line the baking tray with non-stick baking paper.
- If the dough is fatty, take the eggs out of the fridge about 1 hour before using them; this will make the dough more pliable.
- Don't taste samples of the dough if it contains raw eggs.

Meringue type cookies
Separate the egg yolks from the egg whites, place the egg whites in a clean, grease-free bowl. If you whisk cold egg white with a pinch of salt, it gets stiff more quickly. Use the beaten egg white right away, as otherwise it will collapse and cannot be beaten stiff again.

Butter
Make sure the butter is soft when beating it, as it can be stirred more easily and quickly and the dough will be more pliable.

Tips for Making Dough

Keeping a supply of lemon zest
Use unwaxed lemons, wash them under hot running water and let them dry. Only grate the lemon zest as the white pith is very bitter. Deep freeze the zest of squeezed lemons as it can be grated later.

How to weigh honey
Put an empty bowl on the scales, reset scales to zero, then put the honey into the bowl and weigh it.

How to melt chocolate
There are two methods:
1. Break the chocolate into small pieces, add some liquid or butter and melt in a bowl over a bain-marie (double boiler) half-filled with water while continuously stirring.
2. Pour hot water over the crumbled chocolate, let rest for 5 minutes, pour off the excess water except for ½ tbsp, stir till smooth, then use immediately.

How to make crumbly cookie dough more pliable
Fold in 1-2 tbsp milk or 1 small beaten egg white, then knead until dough sticks together.

Chilling the dough
Flatten the dough and wrap it in a clear plastic storage bag or clingfilm. This way the dough chills quickly but doesn't dry out.

Tips for Rolling out Dough and Cutting out Shapes

Useful tips
- Take chilled fatty doughs out of the refrigerator 15-30 minutes before handling them.
- Divide the dough into portions and roll them out on a lightly floured surface. Wrap leftover dough in clingfilm and chill.
- To make sure that the cookies are evenly thin, lay 2 flat, equally thick, pieces of wood on each side of the dough when rolling it out.
- After rolling out the dough on lightly floured work surface or a thin layer of sugar, lift it occasionally from the work surface with a spatula, especially before cutting out shapes from the dough.

Cutting out shapes with cookie cutters
To cut out as many cookies as possible, place the cutters close together. Take the remaining dough and knead lightly, then roll out on a lightly floured work surface again. Dip the cookie cutters occasionally into the flour or sugar so as to be able to remove the cookies from the cutters more easily.

Tips for Rolling out Dough and Cutting out Shapes

Decorating cookies
Make indentations across the top of the cookies with the back of a knife, brush with egg yolk, chill briefly, then bake (see Mailänderli recipe on page 10).

Rolling out dough for meringue type cookie dough,
such as little Swiss brownies (Brunsli) and cinnamon stars (Zimtsterne). Roll out the dough between two sheets of a clear plastic storage bag that has been cut open or on non-stick baking paper, dip the cookie cutter in a little sugar so it's easier to remove the dough from the cutter. Wash the sticky cookie cutters every now and then to prevent dough from sticking to the corners of the cutter.

A faster way to make cookies
You can shape many cookie doughs into rolls, such as Mailänderli (see page 10). Refrigerate the dough, then cut into thick slices while turning the roll every now and then to get round cookies. You may chill the cookies before baking.

Cutting out paper measurements
This is very useful for making rolls the same length, such as crescent cookies (Kipferl), horn-shaped (Hörnchen) or pretzel-shaped (Bretzeli) cookies, aniseed cookies (Chräberli), etc.

Making rosettes of chocolate
Pour the melted icing on a baking sheet, then spread it with a spatula until layer is approx, ½mm / very thin. Leave to dry a little, then produce rosettes of chocolate by paring away the surface with a spatula. Use for garnishing the Toblerone brownies (see page 86).

The variety of ovens available in Switzerland is quite extensive, ranging from gas to electric and convection ovens. Some Swiss still have a gas oven, but the majority use an electric convection/impingement oven.

The temperatures given in the recipes should be taken as reference points, as they may slightly vary depending on the oven you use. So write down next to your recipe the exact baking time with which you obtained a good result.

Pre-heating the oven

Electric and gas ovens with different temperature levels can be easily adjusted. They are equipped with a thermostat that regulates the temperature automatically.

Pre-heat the oven so that the heat is evenly distributed, which will give good baking results. Always pre-heat the oven unless otherwise stated.

- An electric oven reaches 200-250°C / 400-475°F in 10-15 minutes.
- A gas oven reaches the same temperature within 5-7 minutes.

Baking sheets

The baking result depends on the material and the coating of the baking tray. You may want to write down your experience and observations next to the recipe.

Oven and Baking Tips

Convection and impingement ovens
In the convection oven a fan continuously moves hot air throughout the baking chamber. The pre-heating time is about 10 minutes. In the impingement oven a fan makes hot air constantly circulate in the oven. That's the reason why the pre-heating time is reduced to about 5 minutes.
- Reduce the baking temperature by 20°C / 30°F when using either a convection or an impingement oven.
- Bake several trays at a time to make full use of your oven space and to save energy and time. When baking 2-3 trays at a time, the baking time may be a bit longer, though.
- Important: cookies may turn golden brown more quickly when baked in a convection or impingement oven than in a conventional one, but they do hardly get any darker. Don't take the baking tray out of the oven too early.

What to do if the cookies bake unevenly?
- Make sure the cookies are evenly thick and shaped before baking them.
- The bottom heat in gas ovens may be stronger than in electric ones. Move the baking sheet one rack level higher if the cookies turn too dark.
- Check the temperature in the oven with a thermometer comparing with the built-in oven thermometer.
- If possible, use the baking trays that belong to the oven.
- Make sure the baking tray is properly placed in the oven and touches the back of the oven.
- Don't open the oven door unless absolutely necessary so as not to create a draught.
- Ovens occasionally bake unevenly. If this happens, turn the baking sheet 180 degrees halfway through baking time.

Tips
- Line the baking tray with baking paper; it can be used several times.
- Place the cookies on several sheets of baking paper, then transfer them one at a time to the baking tray just before baking them.
- Rinse warm baking tray under cold water before putting the cookies on it.
- Place cookies that shouldn't be baked on baking paper, like Chräbeli, on the greased back of a baking tray. Then they can be removed more easily.
- Generously space the cookies apart on the baking tray.
- Chill the baking tray with fatty cookies for about 15 minutes before baking.
- Allow the cookies to cool on the baking tray for 3-4 minutes after baking, as they can be removed more easily and are less likely to break.

Storing
• Store each variety of cookie separately so the flavours don't mix.
• Put crunchy cookies in airtight tins and keep in a cool and dry place.
• Keep meringue type cookies and aniseed cookies in a cool place. If stored in a cookie tin, don't close it tightly.
• Store the cookies in the freezer if you want to keep them for a long time.

Storing cookies
You can also use preserving and jam jars to store cookies for a short time, especially smaller portions.

Freezing ingredients and dough
• You can freeze nuts, whole or ground, for about 3 months.
• Use a cutter, a kitchen appliance, or similar to finely grind frozen nuts or almonds.
• Butter can be frozen for about 1 month; put in the refrigerator to thaw.
• Candied fruits in packages can be stored in the freezer for about 2 months.
• Doughs keep for 4-6 weeks if stored in an airtight plastic bag in the freezer.
• To thaw, leave the dough in the fridge overnight or at room temperature for 2-3 hours.

How to freeze fresh egg yolk or egg white
Put in small plastic containers, yoghurt containers or jars. Write down the number of eggs it contains and the date when stored on a label. Eggs can be stored in the freezer for about 3 months. To thaw, put in the fridge.

Freezing cookies
• All cookies can be stored in the freezer except for macaroons as they become soft and chewy.
• Once cooled, put the cookies in tin and plastic containers or plastic bags and label them. They can be stored in the freezer for 1-2 months.
• To thaw, put the cookies on a plate and wait for about 30 minutes.
• Ice and decorate the cookies only after thawing.

Freezing fatty cookies
Separate the cookies according to variety and if possible, place each kind in a separate container. Separate the layers by putting baking paper or similar between them. They'll keep in the freezer for about 3-4 weeks at the most.

Weights & Measures

Converting grams (g), kilograms (kg), ounces (oz), pounds (lb)

From Metric

Known	Multiply by	To get
grams (g)	0.035	ounces (oz)
kilograms (kg)	2.2	pounds (lb)

To Metric

Known	Multiply by	To get
ounces (oz)	28.35	grams (g)
pounds (lb)	0.45	kilograms (g)

Tablespoons (tbsp) and teaspoons (tsp)

The sizes of tablespoons (tbsp) and teaspoons (tsp) differ from country to country. While the standard tablespoon in Switzerland holds 15 ml, the British one holds 17.7 ml and the American one 14.2 ml. The capacity of the standard Swiss teaspoon is 5 ml, whereas the British one holds 5.9 ml and the American one 4.9 ml.

1 flat tbsp = 3 flat tsp

Weights & Measures

Converting weight to volume: grams (g) to cups and vice versa

Since the ingredients used in baking differ in weight, there is no formula to convert weight to volume and vice versa. So if you wish to convert grams and kilograms into cups (US) or vice versa, you have to convert the weight for each ingredient separately. The conversions used in the recipes are based on the website www.onlineconversion.com. Since they aren't exact, the measurements in the recipes have been rounded up or down. Be careful with flour, as there are big differences between the different kinds.

In the following you'll find a list of the most important ingredients from grams to cups. 100g of each of the ingredients listed below equals 3¼ oz.

Almonds, chopped	100g	¾ cup
Almonds, ground	100g	1⅛ cups
Almonds, whole	100g	⅔ cup
Butter	100g	½ cup
Candied peel (orange, lemon)	100g	¾ cup
Chocolate, crumbled	100g	½ cup
Chocolate powder	100g	¾ cup
Currants	100g	⅔ cup
Figs, dried	100g	⅔ cup
Flour, buckwheat	100g	½ cup
Flour, plain	100g	¾ cup
Flour, wholemeal	100g	¾ cup
Hazelnuts, chopped	100g	¾ cup
Hazelnuts, ground	100g	1⅛ cups
Hazelnuts, whole	100g	⅔ cup
Honey, acacia	100g	¼ cup
Jam / jelly	100g	½ cup
Pears, dried	100g	⅔ cup
Raisins	100g	⅔ cup
Sugar, granulated / cane	100g	½ cup
Sugar, icing / powdered	100g	¾ cup
Sultanas	100g	⅔ cup
Zwieback	100g	1 cup
Walnuts, chopped	100g	¾ cup
Walnuts, ground	100g	1⅛ cups
Walnuts, whole	100g	⅔ cup

Weights & Measures

Converting litres (l), millilitres (ml), pints (pt), fluid ounces (fluid oz)

From Metric

Known	Multiply by	To get
litres (l)	1.76	pints (pt), UK
litres (l)	2.11	pints (pt), US liquid
millilitres (ml)	0.0352	ounces (oz), UK liquid
millilitres (ml)	0.0338	ounces (oz), US liquid
millilitres (ml)	0.0042	cups

To Metric

Known	Multiply by	To get
pints (pt), UK	0.57	litres (l)
pints (pt), US liquid	0.47	litres (l)
ounces (oz), UK liquid	28.41	millilitres (ml)
ounces (oz), US liquid	29.57	millilitres (ml)
cups	236.59	millilitres (ml)

Converting millimetres (mm), centimetres (cm), inches (in)

From Metric

Known	Multiply by	To get
millimetres (mm)	0.039	inches (in)
centimetres (cm)	0.394	inches (in)

To Metric

Known	Multiply by	To get
inches (in)	25.4	millimetres (mm)
inches (in)	2.54	centimetres (cm)

Oven Temperatures

Converting Centigrade (°C) to Fahrenheit (°F) and Gas Marks (Gas Mk)

Centigrade (°C)	Fahrenheit (°F)	Gas Mark	Description
110	225	¼	Very cool / very slow
120	250	½	slow
140	275	1	slow
150	300	2	cool
170	325	3	cool
180	350	4	very moderate
190	375	5	moderate
200	400	6	moderate
220	425	7	moderately hot
230	450	8	hot
250	475	9	very hot

Notes

Notes

Index

Index

About Bergli Books

Bergli Books publishes, promotes and distributes books, mostly in English, that focus on living in Switzerland.

Ticking Along with the Swiss
edited by Dianne Dicks, entertaining and informative personal experiences of many 'foreigners' living in Switzerland. ISBN 978-3-9520002-4-3.

Ticking Along Too
edited by Dianne Dicks, has more personal experiences, a mix of social commentary, warm admiration and observations of the Swiss as friends, neighbours and business partners. ISBN 978-3-9520002-1-2.

Ticking Along Free
edited by Dianne Dicks, with more stories about living with the Swiss, this time with some prominent Swiss writers. ISBN 978-3-905252-02-6.

Cupid's Wild Arrows – intercultural romance and its consequences
edited by Dianne Dicks, contains personal experiences of 55 authors living with two worlds in one partnership. ISBN 978-3-9520002-2-9.

Laughing Along with the Swiss
by Paul Bilton has everything you need to know to endear you to the Swiss forever. ISBN 978-3-905252-01-9.

Once Upon an Alp
by Eugene Epstein. A selection of the best stories from this well-known American/Swiss humorist. ISBN 978-3-905252-05-7.

Swiss Me
by Roger Bonner, illustrations by Edi Barth. A collection of playful stories about living with the Swiss by a Swiss/American humorist. ISBN 978-3-905252-11-8.

A Taste of Switzerland
by Sue Style, with over 50 recipes that show the richness of this country's diverse gastronomic cultures. ISBN 978-3-9520002-7-4.

The recipes range from savoury dishes like

- Ziibelewaije (onion tart)
- Ticinese Carnival Risotto
- Chäs-Chüechli/Ramequins au Fromage (cheese pies)
- Cheese Fondue
- Appezöller Rösti (pan-fried potatoes with bacon)
- Älpler Magrone (macaroni with bacon, cream and cheese)
- Capuns (Swiss chard rolls with sausage in cream sauce)
- Rösti
- Papet Vaudois (Vaud sausages with leeks, cream and potatoes)
- Real Raclette

to bread and sweets

- Züpfe (plaited milk loaf)
- Rüebli-Torte (carrot cake)
- Frau Boenheim's Chocolate Mousse
- 'Mama Ruth's' Apple Strudel
- Gâteau aux pruneaux (quetsch plum tart)

Berne – a portrait of Switzerland's federal capital,
of its people, culture and spirit,
by Peter Studer (photographs), Walter Däpp, Bernhard Giger and Peter Krebs. ISBN 978-3-9520002-9-8.

Beyond Chocolate – understanding Swiss culture
by Margaret Oertig-Davidson, an in-depth discussion of the cultural attitudes and values of the Swiss for newcomers and long-term residents. English edition ISBN 978-3-905252-06-4. German edition ISBN 978-3-905252-10-1.

Lifting the Mask – your guide to Basel Fasnacht
by Peter Habicht, illustrations by Fredy Prack. Whether you are a first-time visitor or a life-long enthusiast, here's all you need to know (and more) to enjoy Basel's famous carnival. English edition ISBN 978-3-905252-04-0. German edition ISBN 978-3-905252-09-5.

Culture Smart Switzerland – a quick guide to customs and etiquette
by Kendall Maycock provides crucial insights to business culture to help newcomers navigate their way quickly through Swiss life and society. ISBN 978-3-905252-12-5.

Hoi – your Swiss German survival guide
by Sergio J. Lievano and Nicole Egger, chock-full of cartoons, tips and encouragement to help you learn Swiss German, includes English and Swiss German dictionaries.
English edition ISBN 978-3-905252-13-2.

German edition includes German and Swiss German dictionaries.
ISBN 978-3-905252-14-9.

French edition also includes French and Swiss German dictionaries.
ISBN 978-3-905252-16-3.

More information about Bergli Books can be found at www.bergli.ch.